WHIZ KIDS

CONTENTS

Wherever you see this sign, ask an adult to help you.

WHIZ KIDS
TELL ME HOW SHIPS FLOAT

Written and illustrated by

...RLEY WILLIS

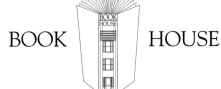

BOOK HOUSE

WILL IT FLOAT OR SINK?

Some objects float.
Some objects sink.
Some objects float so low
in the water that they look
like they are sinking.

A pencil floats.
A fork sinks.
A lemon floats
low in the water.

6

READY, STEADY, SPLASH!

Fill a large bowl with water and collect some objects to test. Try to find things that are different shapes and sizes – some can be heavy and some light. Look for things made from different materials. Before you drop each one in the water, guess if it will sink or float.
Are you right?

SPLASH!

PLOP!

7

ARE FLOATERS BIG OR SMALL?

If an object is light,
it will float.
It can be big or small.

FLOATERS AND SINKERS

Golf balls and ping-pong balls are the
same shape and size. If you drop them
in water, one sinks and the other floats.
The golf ball is small but heavy – it sinks.
The ping-pong ball is small but light – it floats.

WHY DOES IT FLOAT?

A football is
much bigger than
a golf ball, but
the football is light,
so it floats.

A FOOTBALL IS BIG, BUT
IT FLOATS!

9

CAN I FLOAT?

The air inside your body
helps you float.
Air makes you lighter.

When something
is filled with air,
it floats.

BREATHE IN

We breathe with
our lungs. As you
breathe in, you fill
your lungs with air.
The air inside you
helps you float in
the same way
that air-filled
arm bands do.

your
lungs

10

SEE FOR YOURSELF

Take two arm bands, but
only blow up one of them.
Now try to push them both
under the water.
It's hard to push the arm band
that is full of air underwater.

11

WHY DO THINGS FLOAT?

When something falls into water,
the water tries to push it
back out again.
The water's push
is called upthrust.

If an object floats,
it's hard to push it
underwater.

THE UPTHRUST
KEEPS PUSHING
IT OUT AGAIN!

If an object is light, the upthrust can push it back up to the top of the water – it floats.

GOING UP?

A block of wood floats. You can make it sink by putting some coins on it. If you flick the coins off one by one, it will float again. The wood hasn't moved by itself – the water's upthrust has pushed it back up to the top of the water.

WHY DO STONES SINK?

A stone sinks because it is heavy.
The upthrust tries to push it
back up, but the stone
weighs too much.

The upthrust is
not strong enough
to push the stone up
to the top of the water.

AN APPLE
IS LIGHT!

A STONE
IS HEAVY!

BIG STONES SINK!

All stones sink because they are too heavy to float.

SMALL STONES SINK!

15

WHY DID THE BATH OVERFLOW?

If you put too much water in the bath, it will overflow when you get in.

SEE FOR YOURSELF

Half fill the bath.
Mark the water level
with a crayon.
Now climb in.
What happens to
the water level?

16

When you get into a bath,
you take up some of the water's space.
Your body pushes the bathwater
out of its way.
As you get in,
the water level rises.

When any object is put
into water, it pushes the
water out of its way.
The water and the object
can't both be in the same
place at the same time,
so the water level rises.

Do Icebergs Sink or Float?

An iceberg is like a mountain of ice that floats in the sea.
Only the top of an iceberg can be seen – most of it is underwater.

SEE HOW IT FLOATS

Half fill a glass with water. Now drop in an ice cube. See how much of it floats below the water.
This is exactly how a huge iceberg looks as it floats in the sea.

18

WHOOSH!

If an object is light, it will float. Ice floats, but just barely – it floats very low in the water.
This is why so much of an iceberg is hidden underwater.

19

IF STONES SINK, WHY DO SHIPS FLOAT?

A ship made of steel is very heavy,
but its shape helps it float.
The hollow space inside a ship
looks empty, but it is full of air.
The air inside the ship
makes it lighter and
helps it float.

DOES IT WORK?

Fill a bowl with water.
Find some small metal
objects like keys, coins,
forks or spoons.
Drop them in the water
and they will sink.
Place a large cooking
pot in the water
and it floats.
The pot is heavier
– why does it float?

(The air inside the pot
makes it light enough
to float.)

21

IS THE SHAPE IMPORTANT?

A boat's shape takes up
a lot of space in the water.
The boat pushes lots of water
out of its way.

Pushing so much water aside
makes more upthrust.
The water's upthrust
is so strong that
the boat floats.

CAN YOU MAKE IT FLOAT?

You will need: A bowl of water
Some modelling clay made into two large balls
A key

1. Make one ball of modelling clay into a cupped boat shape and place it carefully in the water.
2. Now put the other ball of modelling clay in the water.
3. One sinks and one floats – why?

The boat shape floats because it is lighter (it's full of air). The boat shape makes more upthrust than the ball of modelling clay.

Now place the key very gently in your boat. Can you make the key float too?

NOW IT FLOATS!

23

WHY DO BOATS SINK?

A boat with a heavy load floats low in the water.
A boat that is overloaded floats too low in the water.
If water comes into the boat, it will sink.

This boat weighs too much, so it is too low in the water. When water comes into the boat, the boat gets heavier and sinks.

A special mark on the side of a ship shows if it is too low in the water. The mark is called the Plimsoll line.

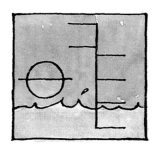

HOW MUCH IS TOO MUCH?

You will need: A small plastic box
(this is your boat)
A crayon
Some pebbles

1. Float the 'boat' in water. Use the crayon to mark how high the water comes up its side.
2. Place some pebbles in the boat.
3. Mark the water level again.
4. Slowly add more pebbles. The boat gets lower and lower. How many pebbles sink the boat?

WE'RE SINKING!

25

WHAT FLOATS AND SINKS?

A submarine can float and sink.
A submarine is a ship
that can travel on water
or underneath it.
It must be waterproof
to keep water out
when it dives underwater.

A submarine has to carry
bottles of air on board
or its crew will run out of
air to breathe.

SOME SUBMARINES
CAN STAY UNDERWATER
FOR MONTHS!

How Do Submarines Work?

A submarine can change how much it weighs. This makes it rise or sink in the water.

Fill one balloon with water and another with air.
Can you feel the difference?

BALLAST TANKS

These are special tanks inside a submarine. By filling them with water, the submarine gets heavier. By filling them with air, it gets lighter.

THIS BALLOON IS LIGHT — IT'S FULL OF AIR!

THIS BALLOON IS HEAVY — IT'S FULL OF WATER!

GOING DOWN

The tanks are flooded with water to make the submarine too heavy to float. It can then dive underwater.

GOING UP

Air is pumped back into the tanks to force the water out. The air in the tanks makes the submarine light enough to float. It rises to the top of the water again.

RAISE THE SUBMARINE

You will need: A plastic bottle
A piece of plastic tubing

1. Fill the bottle with water.
2. Put one end of the tube inside it.
3. Place it carefully into a bowl of water.
4. Slowly blow into the tube to make the bottle rise.

This is how a submarine works.

GLOSSARY

ballast tanks	Special tanks that can be made heavier or lighter to make a submarine sink or rise.
float	When an object rests on top of water.
heavy	When an object weighs a lot.
hollow	When an object has empty space inside it.
iceberg	A huge piece of ice that floats in the sea.
light	When an object weighs very little.
lungs	The parts of your body that fill with air when you breathe.
overflow	When something spills over the top of its container.
overload	When too much is carried.
Plimsoll line	A mark on the side of a ship to show if it is overloaded.
sink	When an object disappears below the water.
submarine	A ship that can travel on or under water.
upthrust	The force when water pushes upward.
water level	The height of the water.
waterproof	Sealed to keep water on the outside.